Hayfield Road

Nine Hundred Years of an Oxford Neighbourhood

by
Catherine Robinson
and
Elspeth Buxton

1993

Hayfields Hut from the south, sketched in pencil, c. 1860

Prehistoric Hayfield Road

In Jurassic times (150 million years ago, more or less) Oxfordshire, like much of southern England, was under water, covered by the Tethyan Sea. Our link with those times is the skeleton of *Eustreptospondylus*, discovered in 1871 in a brick pit just north of Bainton Road. The corpse of this carnosaur drifted out to sea and sank, becoming incorporated in a bed of Oxford Clay, where it was found by the bookseller and amateur geologist James Parker. The skeleton is now in the University Museum, the most intact specimen in western Europe.

The first evidence of human settlement in the area dates back 4,000 years. Implements from the Bronze Age (c. 2000-1500 BC) have been found in Aristotle Lane, and early Bronze Age pots have been found in graves in Polstead Road. On Port Meadow, to the north-west of the Trap Grounds, there are signs of six "ring ditches", probably funeral barrows. One of them, known as Round Hill, was excavated in 1842 by Sheriff Hunt, and later by T.E. Lawrence ("Lawrence of Arabia"), when he was a schoolboy living in Polstead Road. We have no record of what, if anything, they found.

Densely wooded as it was in prehistoric times, the meadow would not have been so liable to flooding as it is now. In the middle Iron Age (about 350 to 50 BC) there were three small farmsteads due west of the Bronze Age sites, around which a number of paddocks were grouped. The evidence can be seen from the air in dry summers, when the boundaries of the prehistoric sites show up as a darker green than the surrounding areas.

The Romans were here too: evidence of a Roman settlement has been found in Chalfont Road and Polstead Road, and just west of St Margaret's Church. Nothing is known of the area in the Dark Ages, but Port Meadow is referred to in the Domesday Book (1086) as the place where "all the burgesses [or Freemen] of Oxford have a pasture outside the city wall in common".

A road by any other name ...

It is on Benjamin Cole's map of Port Meadow, made in 1720, that Hayfield Road is first documented. He called it "The Upper Way to Wolvercote". (The lower road ran from Aristotle Lane across Port Meadow.) Wolvercote has existed for at least 900 years and so, presumably, has "the Upper Way". On maps of St Giles, dated 1769, our road is called "Old Road". Several references in *Jackson's Oxford Journal* in the eighteenth century call it "Heyfield's Hutt" or "Hayfield's Hut", taking the name from a cottage on the site of the present Anchor Inn. A map of 1832 calls it "the Hat"! On the Ordnance Survey map of 1876, its name is "Heyfield Lane". As late as 1950 the name is spelt "Heyfield" in three advertisements in St Margaret's parish magazine.

All the maps agree that, from the earliest times, the road which was to become known as Hayfield Road took a sharp turn to the left at its northern end, following the line of what is now Frenchay Road. But the chief focus of interest lies at the southern end of the road, where our story really begins.

Houses of refreshment

In the beginning there was a well, situated in what is now the cellar of the house on the corner of Kingston Road and Aristotle Lane. According to the seventeenth-century diarist Anthony Wood, this well "was anciently called Brumman's Well, together with that at Walton, because Brumman le Rich, or de Walton [one of the knights of Robert d'Oilly, the Norman governor of Oxford Castle] lived and owned lands about the said wells". Wood records that in his day the well had become known as Aristotle's Well, because it was a favourite haunt of scholars, walking out from Oxford through the fields in summer.

In 1718 Thomas Hearne recorded in his Journal that there was a house of refreshment near the well, and it is tempting to suppose that he meant the cottage on the site of the present Anchor, which appears on Cole's map of Port Meadow, produced in 1720. Cole called the cottage Heathfields Hutt, but he seems to

Aristotle's Well, sketched in 1889

have mistaken the name, for we know that a man named Heyfield lived there around that time. *Jackson's Oxford Journal* announced on January 24 1778: "On Tuesday last died, aged upwards of 90, Mr Heyfield, who for many years kept the Hutt known by his name in the Road leading from the City to Port Meadow."

At this time the hostelry had, it seems, a rather dubious reputation. *Jackson's Journal* of 25 February 1764 tells us of a game of cards at the Hut in which the eminent Dr Webb, a tooth-drawer, blood-letter, and wig-maker, lost 44 guineas and the mortgage deeds of two houses in St Thomas's. There is a veiled hint that the doctor may have been the victim of a group of card-sharps.

In 1845 the Hut appears as "The Anchor" in Hunt's City of Oxford Directory, which names the landlord as Anthony Harris. By 1852 he had been succeeded by William Dolley, who ran the pub with his wife Charlotte until 1877. He must have been a memorable character, because the inn acquired the affectionate nickname "Dolly's Hut" which it still bears today, even though it was demolished and rebuilt in 1936. Older residents of Hayfield Road remember the original inn as a cosy and cheerful place, with tiny bars and low ceilings ("just like a dolly's hut", recalls one man).

Some time around 1875 a rival establishment seems to have begun business. Thomas Johnson, the lessee of Navigation House, on the canal wharf opposite the Anchor, is described in the Oxford Directory as a "coal and manure merchant and beer retailer". Presumably he and his wife Ann supplied beer to the boatmen and the wharf workers. On the same site were a weighing office, stables for the boatmen's horses, pig sheds, and — somewhat incongruously — a Mission Room. Navigation House, which older residents remember as a tall building whose front door opened directly on to the street, was acquired and demolished in the 1960s by Midland Builders (later UBM), who built what is now Oxford Illustrators on the site of the canal wharf.

❧ Heyfield Hutt Lane ☙

It is hard to imagine a settlement of people existing in Hayfield Road before the present houses were built in 1886-1888. But an article in the *Clarendonian* magazine of 1923, recalling Walton Manor in the 1860s, describes "some very old dilapidated cottages" on the west side of Heyfield Hutt Lane, "the gardens of which extended to the canal".

To discover who lived in these cottages, we have to decipher the faded handwriting of the Census returns for the mid-nineteenth century. The 1841 Census records twelve families living in "Heyfields Hutt" (apart from the family of Anthony Harris, the inn-keeper at the Anchor). The breadwinners consisted of four agricultural labourers, a millwright, a carpenter, a pipe maker, and five boat builders. Joseph Carter, the pipe maker, has left his legacy in the garden of the present number 51, where clay pipes are still dug up till this day. (He probably obtained his materials from Webb's clay pits, on the present site of the Unipart works beyond Bainton Road.) The boat builders, whose birthplaces were not in Oxfordshire, do not appear in the next Census, so it seems that they were itinerant craftsmen, following the canals as they spread across England.

In the Census for 1851, William Dolley appears as the publican of the Anchor, beginning his 26-year reign that was to give the inn the nickname "Dolly's Hut", which still survives today. The rest of the names are illegible. It is tempting to suppose that they might have been itinerant labourers, working on the construction of the LNWR branch line nearby.

By 1861 the community in the cottages had shrunk to four families, headed by two agricultural labourers, a French-polisher, and a market gardener. In 1871, for some reason, the population had increased again, and although it included a pig dealer and two small-holders, the presence of two bricklayers and three general labourers reminds us that the fields and meadows of Walton Manor were being fast covered by new housing developments.

By 1881 (in the last Census before the cottages were demolished) the last remaining market gardener is outnumbered by five builder's labourers, a bricklayer, a coal porter, and a "furnace man" (at Lucy's Ironworks?). Interestingly, for the first time, the women's trades are recorded: five are described as laundresses, one as a clothing factory worker, and one, Elizabeth Ayres, is described as a glove maker (not surprisingly, as she came from Stonesfield, the centre of glove-making in Oxfordshire).

❧ The suburb that never was ❧

According to local legend, the present houses in Hayfield Road were built to accommodate railwaymen and their families. Like most legends, this one is half true. As early as October 1865, *Jackson's Oxford Journal* was announcing that "the Great Western Railway have taken a lease on Corporation land at Cripley Meadow for the removal there from Paddington of their carriage and wagon factories". St John's College, ever quick to seize an opportunity to make money, foresaw the need for new housing for several hundred artisans and their families, and instructed its architects to draw up plans for "the requisite residences on college land beyond Heyfield's Hutt". The Journal confidently predicted that "a new suburb will shortly be springing up".

But the developers and the Journal reckoned without the powerful conservative lobby in Oxford. The University, dismayed at the prospect of Oxford becoming a manufacturing town, brought pressure to bear in the right quarters, and the wagon works were eventually built in Swindon instead.

Plans for a new suburb of "sound and healthy dwellings, to be let at moderate rents" were shelved for 20 years, and when eventually they were revived, in 1885, only one road — our own — was actually built. All this explains why Hayfield Road looks so oddly out of context among the Victorian Gothic villas of North Oxford: it was originally intended to be part of a grid of identical streets, consisting of "plain, substantial cottages".

In 1885 St John's agreed to lease land in Heyfield Road to the Oxford Industrial and Provident Land and Building Society, which would build terraced houses, to the design of the College architect, for lease to its members at prices ranging from £170 to £176. At the same time, the Canal Company was improving the wharf, and St John's was transforming The Hut public house into what the *Journal* described as "a picturesque wayside inn".

On 13 October 1888 the *Journal* reported that the Oxford Industrial and Provident ("that flourishing and useful society") had completed the building of "a whole street of model artisans' dwellings". Most of the leases were taken by tradespeople who lived elsewhere and sub-let the houses to poorer families. The Blencowe sisters, for instance, the four daughters of the baker in Kingston Road, acquired one house each in Hayfield Road, for sub-letting. Only ten of the residents recorded in the 1891 census were lease-holders; most of them were carpenters, though there was one police constable (whom we shall meet again). The rest, who sub-let for rents of approximately 4s 6d a week, were a mixture of printers, labourers, and gardeners — and only seven railway workers.

"Sound and healthy dwellings, to let at moderate rents"

The street consists of nine blocks of neat red-brick houses, with eight or ten dwellings in each block. The houses are of identical design, except that for some reason numbers 1-43 are five feet wider than numbers 45-90. The uniformity of design is relieved by the stone mouldings over the front doors which were the trade mark of H. Wilkinson Moore, the architect: oak leaves intertwined with ivy, cherries and plums wreathed with roses, and vine leaves crowned with pineapples. The houses are of sound construction and pleasing proportions.

Inside, each house consisted originally of a small front parlour, kept for "best", and a larger back room, where there was a fireplace with an oven. Clothes were washed in a copper in the scullery, and the family, lacking a bathroom, would use a tin bath in front of the fire. Upstairs, each of the three bedrooms had a fireplace with fancy iron mouldings. The entrance to the lavatory was outside in the back yard.

In the back gardens people kept pigs, hens, ferrets, and racing pigeons. In 1896 Mr W.T. Walker of 37 Chalfont Road complained to St John's about the pigs kept in the adjacent gardens of Hayfield Road: "It is not only the keeping of pigs that is a nuisance, but also the killing. Two were killed last year, close to my garden, a pleasant sort of thing to have close to you!"

❧ Hard times: Oxford in the late 1880s ☙

Contemporary editions of *The Oxford Times* (preserved in the City Library) give us a vivid picture of life in Oxford at the time when the Hayfield Road houses were being built. The year 1886, the local paper recorded, was "full of anxiety for all classes of people, and especially among the poor, who have laboured under quite exceptional distress". Arctic weather in the winter of 1886 led the Corporation to set up soup kitchens and job-creation schemes, in which gangs of men worked on the widening of Woodstock Road and Banbury Road (*"reckless and extravagant expenditure"*, snorted a group of Summertown ratepayers in a letter to *The Oxford Times*). In December John Ryan, a tramp, was sentenced by the Magistrates to seven days' hard labour for begging in St Margaret's Road.

The country was overshadowed by the prospect of war. "The continent at this moment is one vast armed camp", recorded *The Oxford Times* in January 1887. "Russia, Germany, France, Italy, Austria, and Turkey are rapidly getting their armies on a war footing. Some ten million men are ready for action ...". A retrospective account of the dying year reads: "Tensions in the Balkans nearly precipitated Europe into a huge and bloody war, the end of which no man could have foreseen."

At home, "all political circles were ablaze and excitement rose to fever pitch" when Mr Gladstone introduced his scheme for Home Rule for Ireland. His government was defeated on the issue in June 1887, Gladstone resigned, and a general election produced a new administration, led by Lord Salisbury. Oxford's sitting Conservative MP, Mr Hall, was so popular (the Primrose League having assiduously courted working men's votes) that the Liberals did not bother to put up a candidate against him. The Socialists, not yet organised into a political party, were already active in the city: *The Oxford Times* records a meeting of the Oxford Socialist League in the Temperance Hall in Pembroke Street to hear a lecture on "The Origin of Capital".

Some people had their private worries. In January 1887, Elias Nelms, cab-proprietor (trading on the site of the present Aladdin Garage in Hayfield Road), was sued for breach of promise of marriage by Miss Sarah Rayner, a housemaid at Tew Park.

If it all got too much, you could always emigrate to America. *The Oxford Times* advertised places on the Royal Mail Steamer from Liverpool to New York for £7. Or you could turn to the bottle: Hall's Brewery (owned by the Conservative member of parliament) was advertising "Double Stout for Invalids" at 1s 4d a gallon. The pages of the *Oxford Times* were full of advertisements for patent medicines, such as Thomas's Dandelion, Camomile, and Rhubarb Pills for indigestion (*"beware of spurious imitations"*). Those of a nervous disposition were urged to purchase Dr Bell's Patent Voltaic Belt.

If you lived in Hayfield Road, however, you could not afford to indulge a nervous disposition. Jobs were scarce, families large, and wages low. Many of the men worked as builders' labourers, laid off in the winter months without pay.

Who were they? Where did they come from? How did their wives manage? The copperplate handwriting of the 1891 Census tells us much about their lives.

❧ What the census tells us ☙

The census for 1891, the first taken after the building of the new Hayfield Road was complete, reveals that there were 403 people living in the street: an average of five people per house. There were 180 children under the age of 14 (compared with barely ten today). The largest family in the Road was the Chappells at number 80, with ten children ranging in age from 7 months to 12 years. The eldest Chappell girls rejoiced in the names of Rose, Lillie, Daisy, Violet, and Myrtle.

William Chappell, their father, was a coach wheeler by trade, and was born in Greenwich. Unlike him, most of the breadwinners (54 out of 82) were born in Oxfordshire (as were 52 of their wives). But one astonishing exception to this general tendency was Hira Lal Kumar, a 28-year old widowed journalist, born in India, and living as a lodger at number 38 with John and Elizabeth Mills and their children Harold and Violet!

With one exception (the Post Office Stamper at number 72), Hira Lal Kumar was the only man in Hayfield Road who did not earn his living from a manual trade. The main occupations for men were the following:

- labouring (on building sites or coal yards)   12
- printing (including compositors and type founders)   10
- carpenters/joiners   10
- gardeners   9
- coachmen/grooms   9
- railway workers (mostly porters and signalmen)   7

The rest were mostly bricklayers and tradesmen's porters. Only 21 women are recorded as being in paid employment. Nine, mostly in their teens, were domestic servants (who could expect to earn about £10 a year, unless they lived in *"Wanted: general servant who can do plain cooking; an early riser and abstainer preferred; £24 p.a., all found"*). Three young women, perhaps more enterprising than their sisters, were dressmakers. Virtually no women between the ages of 25 and 45 were in paid employment — obviously they were fully occupied in raising their families. Three older women are recorded as sick nurses, and five as laundresses. Working at home, for the colleges, they would earn about 5s. a week during term-time. Of the boy school-leavers, four were lucky to have apprenticeships (in printing, hosiery, and cobbling); the rest were servants or errand boys.

Links with the past

The earlier canal-side community that existed before the present houses were built had disappeared almost without trace when the old cottages were demolished in 1884. But one link remained, in the person of Agabus Green, a builder's labourer who was born in Cumnor and is recorded as living in "Heyfields Hutt" in 1871 with his wife Ann and their five children. By 1891 Agabus, now aged 60, and Ann, aged 58, were living in the relative comfort of a new house at number 41, with 16-year old Annie — the other five children having left home. St Margaret's Parish Magazine records the death of Agabus Green, "One of the oldest residents in this district" in 1901. One of the first elected sidesmen at St Margaret's, "to which he was loyally devoted", he attended church "with the utmost regularity. He possessed the respect and regard of all who came into contact with him, and his loss is a real one, to his church and his parish."

One other person whose life spanned the two communities was Anthony Harris, the son of Anthony Harris, landlord of The Anchor in the 1840s. Young Anthony married the girl across the street — Sarah Johnson, daughter of Thomas Johnson, the coal and beer merchant at Navigation House on the wharf. In 1881 Anthony, aged 43, was living with his father-in-law, helping in the business. By 1891, he and his family had moved from the far south of the street to the far north, at number 73. He is described as a farmer (presumably on land beyond the canal). Last recorded in Kelly's Street Directory in 1900, he had lived in the road for at least 62 years.

Of the families who moved into the new houses in 1888, however, Ada Tombs held the record for longevity. One year old when the 1891 census was taken, she kept house for her brothers William and Thomas at number 3 all her life, surviving them to die in 1971 at the age of 81. "Cissie", as she was known, worked in a college kitchen. Local people still remember her prim and proper ways ("She scrubbed her front door-step every day of her life"). The canal boatmen used to throw their boots into her garden as they passed, for Tommy the "shoe-snob" to mend, and would collect them on their return journey. She must have seen a lot in her long life: if only someone had interviewed her before she died ...

And if only we had interviewed Miss Winnie Allen, who died at the age of 90 in 1993 at number 40, the house where she was born. The youngest of 10 children, Miss Allen had been apprenticed to a Court dressmaker in London ("and always looked elegant in her youth"), but she returned to Hayfield Road to look after her ageing parents. Of all the people who were born and died in the road, she probably lived the longest.

❧ St Margaret's Church ☙

The records of the parish church reveal what an important role the church played in the social life of the area in the years before the first world war.

In 1882, the parish magazine of St Philip and St James records: "For some years past, an afternoon service has been held in a room at Hayfield's Hut, which must soon be pulled down, owing to projected improvements". Half the rent of the Mission Room had been paid by the Women's Branch of the Guild of SS Philip and James. A small night school had been held there during the winter months, "at which two or three of the Guild Brethren were teachers". It is not clear whose needs the Mission Room and Night School existed to serve: those of the canal-boat community (which greatly exercised Victorian moralists and philanthropists), or those of the cottagers like Agabus Green. At any event, the demolition of the Mission and the "projected improvements" to Hayfield Road led to the building of St Margaret's Church (a daughter church of Phil and Jim) in 1883/84, and the Working Men's Institute in 1889.

Almost at once, a vigorous parish life began, in which many Hayfield Road people were involved. The early church magazines are full of accounts of Penny Readings, Harvest Festivals, musical entertainments, lantern lectures, and missionary pageants. The Church Lads' Brigade was particularly active, and the magazine carried stirring accounts of the camps and marches and mock battles that the boys enjoyed.

The Sunday School, too, had outings (by charabanc to Shotover, and river steamer to Abingdon), and a grand tea in July and December each year. In the lists of prizes for attendance, many familiar names recur: the Goddards, Shirleys, Tuffreys, Sodens, and so on. (Later, the same names appear under the "Weddings" heading, and we learn that there was much inter-marriage among families in the street.)

Like St Paul's and St Barnabas' in Jericho, St Margaret's was "high", with incense and a choir and catechism classes. Separate Bible classes were held for women and men, and the vicar's wife, Mrs Hartley, held sewing classes for young servant girls. There was a parish library in the vestry (subscription: 3d a year), and a parish invalid chair too, kept at number 22 in the charge of Mrs Dawson, from whom it could be hired at 3d an hour.

There was a short-lived Literary and Scientific Society, which heard lectures on subjects such as "Italian Masters in the National Gallery". Far more enduring was the St Margaret's Horticultural Society, whose grand show was held in August each year, in the vicarage garden. The Duke of Marlborough (who owned land hereabouts) presented the prizes on several occasions. The Committee was illustrious indeed: in 1905, the President was the Revd Mr Hartley, and Vice-Presidents included Mr G. Morrell

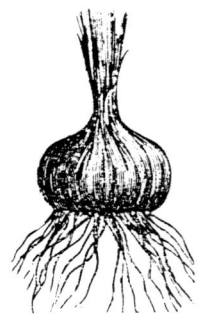

(MP), Sir William Herschel, Mr S. Acott, and Sir Walter and Lady Grey. There were social events as well as displays of prize onions: in 1902, for instance, a Concert and Dance, to the accompaniment of a Banjo and Mandolin Band.

Charitable duties were not forgotten. The collection on Ash Wednesday was regularly given to the Penitentiary in Holywell (with which the parish seems to have had some sort of link). In April 1890 the proceeds of one of the many Sales of Work ("plain and fancy needlework, soldiers' clothing, etc.") were given to the Indian Famine Fund.

As for the poor closer to home, their needs were catered for by Miss Threlkeld, the Church's District Visitor for Hayfield Road, and by the Relief Committee, which was very active in the years before the first world war. In 1911 it appealed for "gifts of men's clothes suitable for emigrants to Australia" and "a purchaser for the following items, to help their owner raise funds towards emigration: a treadle sewing machine, a banjo, and a child's mail-cart". One family who took their chances in Australia were the Pitmans from number 22.

We do not know how many men the Committee managed to train in farm work "without wage, with a view to fitting them for emigration", but we may be sure that their departure would have left a void in this close-knit community. One poignant entry in the parish magazine in 1901 illustrates just how close-knit it was. Referring to the recent terrible loss of HMS Cobra with all hands on board, it mourns the drowning of 23-year old Leonard Tuffrey of Hayfield Road (*"present at our recent Flower Show"*). Fourteen years later, black-edged funeral cards began to appear in the front windows of Hayfield Road as young men of the Oxon and Bucks Light Infantry died on the fields of Flanders. Their names are recorded on the war memorial on the corner of St Margaret's Road.

The Working Men's Institute

In 1889 some of the well-to-do parishioners of St Philip and St James invited subscriptions for the building of a Working Men's Institute, "to provide rational amusement and instruction for working men of any creed, sect, or opinions, who may thus be kept out of public houses" (according to a letter from one local gentleman to another, soliciting a contribution in August 1889). He added, "The working men are taking it up and raising money themselves."

Enough money was raised to buy from St John's College the 99-year lease of a plot of land on which to build a three-storey parish institute. It was the first house to be built in Polstead Road. The ground floor housed a Working Men's Club, open each day from 2pm. There was a spacious Games Room for cards, darts, chess, and dominoes. Off this was a washroom and a bathroom (a boon to the men of Hayfield Road, whose houses had been built without baths). Running from one end of the building to the other was the billiards room, said to be the finest of its kind in Oxford, with raised cushioned seating round the table. The Oxford Billiard League held its championship matches here. A

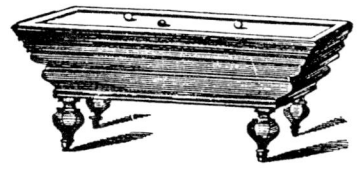

library contained all kinds of books and numerous periodicals. In every room there was a blazing coal fire. Everything in the Club was of good quality: real silver cutlery and real china.

The Club was a flourishing concern. It usually numbered about 150 members, who had to apply for admission and be sponsored. The heyday of the Club was the 1930s. During this decade a parishioner, Mrs Rashdall, gave the money to build a church hall projecting out from the back of the Institute. But after the war there began a decline of the Working Men's Club; even the billiard saloon lost its popularity. Part of the reason was the advent of television and part, perhaps, was the refusal of the Trustees to allow the sale of alcohol on the premises.

So St Margaret's Institute was built not just for the church or for the parish in the narrow sense, but for the use of the community as a whole — as, indeed, it is still used today.

❧ Before the first world war: the life and times ❧ of the Goddard family

A vivid record of life in Hayfield Road before the first world war has been given to us by Miss Florrie Goddard, a relative of the Goddards who moved into 53 Hayfield Road when it was first built. Edwin Goddard (born 1856) was a police constable. His wife Esther worked hard, cleaning and caretaking in big North Oxford houses when their owners went away for the summer holidays. She would take the smallest of her 8 children with her and, when they were old enough, the boys too used to go round the houses in Chalfont Road before school to light fires and clean shoes. They earned one shilling a week from their "morning places", which they had to put in the bank. The children went to Phil and Jim's School in Leckford Road, and the family attended St Margaret's Church.

Edwin Goddard had been born at the Nut Tree Inn at Murcott on Otmoor, and never forgot his country origins. He had a half-share in a cow on Port Meadow, and some rough shooting on Boar's Hill, and several allotments in Marston Ferry Road. There was often rabbit pie for dinner, and one of the children would besent to Warburton's in The Friars to sell the skin for twopence. Mr Goddard kept ducks, hens, rabbits, ferrets, and bees in the back garden of number 53. Florrie Goddard recalls that there was always plenty of milk from the cow, and Mrs Goddard used to make butter from the cream by shaking it in a big glass sweet bottle. With so many mouths to feed, one of the boys used to be sent down to Butler's in Park End Street with a sack to fill up with bread, as it was a ha'penny cheaper there.

Since the canal ran at the bottom of the garden, the boys were each given a shilling as soon as they could swim across it and back. Florrie remembers calling at the house one day with her mother. They pushed open the front door and went in. Suddenly all the boys came running in from the garden with no clothes on, straight from their swim in the canal. Florrie's mother was horrified that her daughter should see all those naked boys!

One unforgettable night PC Goddard, returning home up Walton Street in the early hours of the morning, discovered a fire in the Oxford University Press. He gave the alarm, and little damage was done. Next day the Printer sent for him to thank him, and asked if he could offer him something as a reward. PC Goddard said he had four sons at home, and would be grateful if jobs could be found for them. So William and Edwin and Herbert and Stan started work at the Press, where they stayed all their working lives, like several other residents of Hayfield Road.

❦ Between the wars ❧

"Hayfield Road was like one big family in the old days." Listening to the stories of residents whose memories go back 70 or even 80 years, one hears this comment again and again. *"You couldn't lead a double life in Hayfield Road,"* one lady recalls. *"We all knew one another's business."* Everyone remembers it as a neighbourly community. On summer evenings, people would put chairs out on the pavement and sit gossiping outside their front doors, while the children played in the dusk. "We used to throw up our hats to catch bats," one man recalls. "What we used to sing was: Bat! Bat! Come into my hat!"

Growing up in Hayfield Road

Childhood was short in the years between the wars — the school-leaving age was 14 — and money was short, too. But the children of Hayfield Road knew how to enjoy themselves. "In the school holidays, we played on Port Meadow from dawn to dusk ... We fished for newts with a worm on the end of a string ... We used to put ha'pennies on the railway line, so the trains would flatten them and make them look like pennies ... We had bonfires and roasted potatoes ... We went birds-nesting along the railway line, where Mr Tuffrey did his carpet-beating. All the linnets' nests

along the railway line were lined with fluff from the carpets ... When the Fair Rosamund came along on the way to Woodstock, we knew it was time to go home for lunch. When the fish train came by from Grimsby at 8 pm, that was the signal to go home to bed."

The Hayfield Road children had their own cricket team, captained by Molly Harris ("the best cricketer of them all," everyone agrees). They played on the rec against teams from Jericho. "We could never afford new equipment. But Mr Kidd, the bank manager from Chalfont Road, used to pay us to give him batting practice. If we bowled him out, he gave us 6d, or an old leather ball."

In the street, the girls played with hoops in winter, and spinning tops in summer. There was skipping all the year round. The boys used to "borrow" the parish bath chair from the Institute, and give each other rides in it. Everyone enjoyed the sport of tying people's front-door knobs together and then knocking on the doors, or tying a length of string to a purse and then hiding down an alleyway. "When someone came along and tried to pick it up, we used to pull on the string and the purse would jerk away."

There was more decorous amusement on Sunday evenings, when "we went walking with our parents to Wytham or Wolvercote, sometimes as far as Jacob's Ladder [up the canal, beyond Wolvercote] to see the cowslips and fritillaries". And on Monday evenings there was a Girls' Happy Hour at the Institute, when they made rugs and toy theatres.

But the children of Hayfield Road were quite capable of organising their own entertainments. Edie Dean got all the children to put on a show. "We practised every night under her lamp-post, and when we were ready, we gave a performance at the Institute. The money was given to a home for blind children ... Edie was a nice-looking girl. Later she climbed out of her bedroom window and ran away from home. She went to London and became a film star. She came back to visit Hayfield Road a few times. We were all very impressed by her leopard-skin coat."

"Somehow Mother always coped"

If children in Hayfield Road in the 1920s had more freedom than children do today, it is also true that they had more responsibilities. Times were hard, and the young ones were expected to contribute to the household economy. Some earned a few pennies after school by helping to feed and water the canal boatmen's horses in the stables on the wharf; or by fetching beer for the neighbours from the jug and bottle hatch at the Anchor.

"My mother used to shell peas for the colleges. We little ones helped her. She used to get 3s for shelling 100 lb," one man remembers. "She used to send me to buy the bacon bits left in the slicing machine at Sainsbury's on Saturday nights, and broken cakes and stale buns (3d for a carrier bag full) from Weeks' Bakery in Paradise Square."

Many families kept pigs (in defiance of St John's) in their back gardens. "There was always a side of bacon hanging in our living room," remembers one lady. The children helped to wash the chitterlings and make the brawn. On wash-days they went down to Navigation House with basins to fetch faggots and peas, cooked on her kitchen range by Mary Harris (wife of Albert, the foreman on the wharf).

In some houses in Hayfield Road, every day (except Sunday) was wash-day. Taking in washing for the colleges was one of the few ways in which women could earn money. Mrs Phipps, a Keble College scout who lived at number 26, used to bring stiff-fronted shirts by the dozen for her neighbours to wash. At number 90, old Mrs Offoway (born a Kimber in Headington Quarry) would toil all week: soaking, scrubbing, mangling, pegging out, ironing, and goffering. But on Sundays she would take off her apron, don a long black cape and an ostrich-feathered hat, and walk all the way to Forest Hill and back to visit her family.

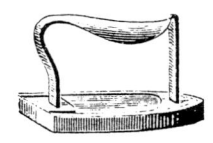

These women were resourceful. Somehow they kept their families clean. (The men took baths at the Institute, but women and children had to go to the pub-

lic wash-house in Paradise Street, or use a tin bath in front of the fire.) They ran a clothing club at the Institute. Although most families paid 4d a week to be on the panel of Dr Woods in Dispensary Road, the women acted as midwives to each other, and were skilled, some of them, in laying out the dead. "If you were ever in trouble," everyone remembers, "there was always someone at hand to help."

"Life was never dull in Hayfield Road"

There was always something happening in the street. On Wednesdays, cows were driven down the road from Wolvercote to the Gloucester Green market. On Saturdays, an Italian hurdy-gurdy man came round, with a monkey that held out a tin for coins.

There was great excitement in September each year, when the show-men from St Giles's Fair camped with their families and horses and caravans in what is now Bainton Road. The children of Hayfield Road, forbidden by their parents to stray too close, were irresistibly drawn to the caravans; but they were disappointed in one respect: "We saw the acrobats and the dancing girls with their hair in curlers. They didn't look a bit glamorous!"

Once a year everyone enjoyed donkey rides and coconut shies at the Radiators Fête. There were grand fancy-dress parties in the street to celebrate George V's silver jubilee, and the coronation of George VI.

On one memorable night, there was a fire at Wooldridge and Simpson's wood-yard near the canal drawbridge. "The sky was all lit up, and you could feel the heat all the way down the street at number 17. Mr Soden ran up and down the street ringing a bell. The wood was lost, but all the horses were saved." And there was the never-forgotten day when Charlie Giles' pig fell in the canal, and everyone in the road helped to haul it out.

The tale of Paraffin Liz

People seem to have been more tolerant of eccentrics in the years between the wars than they are now. There was Paraffin Liz, who lived in a shed on the edge of Port Meadow. Her real name was Miss Dearing (MA Oxon), and she was reputed to have been Librarian at Somerville College. In the 1920s and 1930s she made a living by giving riding lessons to children on the Meadow (allegedly using horses that did not belong to her). "She always rode bare-back. She was a queer old soul, as skinny as a herring. She wore men's boots, and string for a belt, and she had dinner in the Randolph every night."

In another hut near the Meadow lived Daddy Yates, who played the flute. And in a shed named Tingewick in Frog Lane (opposite the end of Frenchay Road) lived Little Mush. He lived alone, isolated from the world by a severe speech impediment. He had a rifle and a spiteful goose ("to ward off the Social"), and three cats, which he adored. Mush used to pick coal from the railway line, and was always filthy. Once his sister persuaded him to go and live with her in Reading, "but she made him have a bath, so he came back the next day". He carried on living in the hut, and Charlie Giles' family carried on taking him Christmas dinner every year until he died.

Charlie Giles himself, at number 72, was a notable character. An inspector with the Great Western Railway, he always wore a flower in his button-hole, and tipped his hat to the roadside crucifix by the church as he cycled home from work ("even when he was drunk"). Believe it or not, he was friendly with Haile Selassie, the exiled Emperor of Abyssinia, who used to wait in Charlie's office for the train; and he was once reported for swearing at the Duke of Marlborough ("but the Duke swore at him first"). Charlie Giles was a rare one. He has been dead for 30 years, but people's faces still break into a smile when his name is mentioned.

Courting days

The delights of playing on the Meadow and teasing Paraffin Liz did not last for ever. As the children of Hayfield Road grew up and left school, their pastimes changed. One lady recalls the days of her first job (at Oxford University Press, where she earned 8s a week for a 13-hour day). "I kept 2s 6d for myself, and went to the Scala in Walton Street twice a week. There were double seats at the back for courting couples. Tickets cost 4d each, and we bought 2d worth of chips. A woman played the piano for the silent films. We liked Tom Mix, and Fu Man Chu, and The Man In The Iron Mask."

She and all the other young people from Hayfield Road used to meet their friends in town at the weekend, parading round "the Bunny Run": from Carfax, up Cornmarket, down George Street, along New Inn Hall Street to Queen Street, and back up to Carfax. There was dancing in the Carfax Assembly Rooms, and ice-skating at the old Majestic Cinema (now MFI) in Botley Road.

War came in 1939, taking away the young men, and bringing new opportunities for young women who otherwise might have been confined to domestic work. The unmarried girls were conscripted to work in the power station in Mill Street, or in Lucy's munitions factory in Walton Well Road. ("My job was weighing shells. I wore a uniform of khaki dungarees with brass buttons. We had good fun.")

Everybody had good fun after the evacuation of Dunkirk, when 45,000 soldiers were camped on Port Meadow, and enterprising local people organised dances at the Institute — three nights a week, dancing to Victor Sylvester records. Imagine being 17 years old in 1940, with enough money for a bit of lipstick, and 45,000 soldiers to dance with!

Shops and trades

The shop at the south end of the street was originally two shops, numbered 4 and 6 Hayfield Road. The first proprietors in 1890 were a butcher and a grocer. In 1904 both premises were being run as a general store and telegraph office by Mrs Restall, wife of the wharfinger and haulier whose business was based on the canal wharf opposite. She was succeeded in 1907 by Richard Hall, who sold furniture in number 4 and household goods in number 6 for 20 years. (His name and business are still proclaimed in

large fading letters on the south wall of number 4.) For the next 25 years Mr and Mrs Berry traded as confectioners at number 4, while next door was a post office. In 1952 both shops were taken over by the Oxford and Swindon Co-op,
which traded there until 1965, when Mr Snowden ("Snowy") opened his animal and garden supplies shop. When he retired in 1965, his young assistant, Lawrence Todd, took over the business, until soaring rents forced him to give up in 1985, whereupon the shop became a delicatessen. Since 1988 Nicholas and Manos Vernicos, ever helpful and smiling, have brought a touch of the Mediterranean to Hayfield Road. We are learning to appreciate Greek food and wine, but some commodities purveyed at the shop have not changed since 1890: local gossip and opinions about the weather!

Next door, the site of the Aladdin Garage was originally the stables for a hansom-cab business run by Elias Nelms, landlord of the Anchor from 1891. The licensee from 1900 to 1907, Sam Ward, kept a livery stables there. Other trades carried on in the street have long since disappeared. According to Kelly's Trade Directory for 1928, Mrs Elizabeth Bassett ran a sweet shop at number 41; Mr and Mrs Henry Johnson presided over an ice-cream parlour at number 49; and Herbert Pacey ran a dairy shop at number 57. Older residents vividly remember taking jugs to the dairy for their mothers, and sitting in the Johnsons' front parlour eating home-made ice cream sprinkled with raspberry juice in two-penny cornets.

❦ The canal and the railway line ❦

No history of Hayfield Road would be complete without an account of the canal and the railway which eventually replaced it. We owe the canal to the demand for coal in the eighteenth century. When coal was first used for domestic heating, it was brought to Oxford from the north-east of England by ship to London and then transferred to barges and brought up the Thames. As demand increased, networks of canals were built to improve distribution. The canal from Coventry reached Banbury in 1778 and on 2 May 1789 it was finished as far as Hayfield's Hut, where a coal wharf was opened. In *Jackson's Oxford Journal* of 3 October 1789, coal prices are given as follows:

COAL WHARF AT HAYFIELDS HUTT

The Oxford Canal being finished and opened at the above wharf, within a quarter of a mile of Oxford, the best coals are sold at the following prices:

Oakthorpe coals, equal in quality to Staffordshire	1s 5d per cwt
Warwickshire	1s 2d per cwt
Staffordshire coke per ton	£1 4s 9d

Considering that sea coal brought from London cost 2s 2d per hundredweight, the savings were obviously considerable. There was great rejoicing on 1 January 1790, when the new City Basin was opened (where Nuffield College now stands). The bells of Oxford rang out and the County Militia band played as the first boats arrived, carrying coal and corn.

In 1792 the Marquis of Buckingham proposed a new cutting, to start at Hayfields Hut and go through Marston, Elsfield, and Woodeaton to Islip and there join a planned canal to London. This never came to anything.

In 1795 the canal was frozen for several weeks (some accounts say six, others ten). The price of coal went up every day and, long before the thaw, supplies had run out. Some enterprising persons took hand-carts to Banbury, but only small supplies of coal could be carried this way, and there was very great hardship. When the thaw came, the prices sank from 4s to 1s 6d a hundredweight.

By the end of the eighteenth century trade was thriving on the canal, and continued to do so for at least 100 years. But it faced

Hayfield Wharf, Oxford Canal, c. 1890, photographed by Henry Taunt. Frank Restall, the wharfinger, stands on the right.

competition from the railway. The line from Didcot to Oxford was built, despite opposition from the University, and opened in June 1844. In September 1850 a line was made to Banbury, but this had little effect on canal traffic until the line was extended northwards to Warwick and Birmingham in February 1853. (While the Banbury line was being built, a tramway was made from what is now Chalfont Road, to take gravel for the laying of the track.)

In January 1907 Port Meadow Halt was opened, on the northern side of the bridge (known as Old Man's Bridge) at Aristotle Lane. No trace of the halt now remains, save the crossing to the allotments. It served the old LNWR line to Bletchley, but seems not to have been economical, for it was closed in 1926.

As for the canal, it never really recovered after the first world war, although coal was still being delivered by horse-drawn boats in the 1930s to what was then a part of Morris Radiators (now Unipart). The lift bridge over the canal was installed in 1930, to be power-operated by a workman from a cabin nearby.

The canal was dredged on Whit Monday each year, and older residents of Hayfield Road have vivid memories of swimming in it. "You could see the bottom from the draw-bridge to the Aristotle Lane bridge, and it was full of perch and roach."

They also remember the narrow boats, "with gleaming brasses, and clothes on the washing lines as white as milk. They were often pulled by bad-tempered mules, which used to escape if they were left untied, and then the men would swear and shout, and we all ran to catch them. Those canal families were tough! I remember the Beauchamps, and the Skinners [Rose and Joseph on the *Friendship*, pulled by their mule Dolly]. The same families would travel up and down the canal all year. The women wore hob-nailed boots, and unloaded coal just like the men. But they put on clean aprons and caps to visit Dolly's Hut."

In 1955 the canal was threatened with closure, but the Canal Protection Society, supported by John Betjeman, won the day. Now the grimy coal boats and their gaudily painted butties have given way to pleasure boats, and we are threatened with a marina (and associated leisure facilities) where the meadow-sweet grows.

To complete our picture of local transport systems, we should note that in 1881 the Oxford Tramway Company was established. Horse-drawn trams took passengers up Walton Street as far as Leckford Road. In 1914 they were replaced by buses with open-top decks and external staircases. The number 3 came up to St Margaret's Road. In the 1980s the mini-bus service started, and has proved to be a great boon.

❧ Port Meadow and the Trap Grounds ❧

Many of us are drawn to Port Meadow for the solitude which its vast empty spaces offer us. But it has not always been so devoid of activity. In the Iron Age there were three small farmsteads there: thatched huts surrounded by paddocks. From early mediaeval times the Freemen of Oxford grazed their horses and cattle there. In 1603 and 1608, cabins were built at the Aristotle Lane entrance, for the isolation of plague victims from the city.

By 1630 the peace of the meadow was being disturbed by the annual Sheriff's Races, which took place for two or three days each summer, and continued until the middle of the nineteenth century. Ladies and gentlemen, horse dealers and pickpockets, scholars and Punch-and-Judy men flocked to the Meadow for the races. They came by coach, on foot, or by boat up the Thames. In *Jackson's Oxford Journal* on 21 June 1788, John Bridge of Hayfield's Hutt was offering stabling for gentlemen's horses at the next meeting.

The races reached the height of their popularity in the eighteenth century, when assemblies and balls were held in the town during Race Week, and hairdressers came specially from London to prepare the ladies' elaborate coiffures. Besides the horse races, there were wrestling and sack races, hog-chasing and "smock-races" (for women in petticoats). In his diary in 1732, Thomas Hearne complained that "Booths and vicious living were there for about seven weeks ... 'tis abominable that Poppet shews and Rope dancing should have been this summer in Oxford for more than two months, to the debauching and corrupting of youth."

Our quiet meadow has also been the site of military activity. In 1644 Charles I slipped out of Oxford by night, across Port Meadow with his army of 5,000 men, making a dash for the West Country. In the 1914-18 war, the meadow was used as an airfield; two of the earliest British pilots were killed in a crash there. In the second world war the exhausted survivors of the Oxfordshire and Buckinghamshire Light Infantry, home from Dunkirk, set up their tents on the meadow.

It is all a far cry from the heron that patrols the banks of the river and the geese that go honking over the rooftops of Hayfield Road on winter nights. To ecologists and naturalists, Port Meadow is a paradise: one of the largest expanses of common land in England, it has never been ploughed, and its plant life has been extensively studied and written about.

Even closer to home, but much less well known, are the Trap Grounds. Once part of a 30-acre mediaeval hay meadow known as Burgess Mead, the Trap Grounds are now reduced to the eight acres of reed-beds and rough land between the canal and the railway line, and Aristotle Lane and the Unipart factory. The area is a treasury of wild life: 32 species of birds breed there, and another 50 species visit the site in winter. Twelve pairs of reed-warblers share the reed-beds with eight pairs of sedge-warblers, six pairs of willow-warblers, and six pairs of reed-bunting. Hiding among the pond-sedge and water-plantain is the elusive water-rail and her mate. Advertising her presence from the tree-tops is the cuckoo, who in 1988 was observed to lay 25 eggs in nests on the Trap Grounds! Brimstone butterflies and marbled whites sun themselves on the meadowsweet, and on very warm days common lizards bask on heaps of stone near the railway line. On April evenings the melancholy call of the rare marsh frog can be heard along the canal bank. All this will be lost if the City Council decides to "develop" the land for offices and light industry. Generations of Hayfield Road people have done their courting and walked their dogs on the Trap Grounds. This unique habitat will disappear under tarmac and concrete if the Residents' Association loses its campaign to protect it.

❧ Epilogue ☙

You could have bought a house in Hayfield Road for £100 after the first world war. You would have been part of a community in which "you could always call on someone". Until the second world war, nobody locked their front door when they went to bed at night. The men drank together and played dominoes at Dolly's Hut on Saturday nights and worked together, many of them, during the week: on the railway, at the Press, or at Lucy's Ironworks. The women sat outside their front doors in the evenings, gossiping. The children roamed Port Meadow and Wytham Wood in the school holidays, with jam sandwiches and a bottle of water for their dinner, the big ones taking care of the little ones. "We were poor," everyone remembers, "but we were happy."

These days £100,000 would not buy you a house in Hayfield Road. We seem to be preoccupied with our kitchen extensions and loft conversions, and we mostly stay behind our own front doors. Residents who were born in nearby villages like Yarnton and Wolvercote are being replaced by newcomers from all over the world. (A survey in 1985 recorded residents from every corner of Britain, as well as Barbados, Belgium, France, India, Iran, Somalia, the USA, and Zambia.) But the older residents are remarkably tolerant of the newcomers, and the old community spirit is still to be seen on occasions like the Centenary Street Party and the celebrations for the ordination of the street's own deacon, the Reverend Freda Beveridge. People are perhaps more inclined to stop for a chat since the road was closed to through traffic in 1985. Gifts of rhubarb from the allotments are still left on front doorsteps (even if the steps are not scrubbed and whitened as faithfully as they once were!). May we never lose the neighbourliness for which Hayfield Road was once renowned.

Appendix: EXTRACT FROM 1891 CENSUS, ref. RG12/1165 3+ HEYFIELD ROAD

NB: *The first-named person in each case is the head of the household; children under 14 (named in italics) are the children of the head of the household unless otherwise stated.*

No.	Name	Age	Occupation/status	Place of birth
1	Thomas Johnson	75	Coal merchant	Wytham
	Jane Johnson	45		Kidlington
	Sarah Simmonds	19	Domestic servant	Kirtlington
	Ernest Tuffrey	16	Coal merchant's assistant	Staffs.
	Leonard Tuffrey	15	Coal merchant's assistant	Staffs.
	+ *Frederick Tuffrey (13), Bert Tuffrey (8)*			
3	William Tombs	28	Carpenter	Headington
	Mary Tombs	26		Oxford
	Anne Davies	56	Nurse	Banbury
	+ *Leah (2), Ada (1), William (2 days)*			
5	Edwin Walker	31	Printer's machine minder	Oxford
	Alice Walker	26		Oxford
	+ *Alice (6), Edwin (4), Percy (2 months)*			
7	William Robinson	40	Gas stoker	Woodstock
	Emily Robinson	38		Oxford
	+ *Nathaniel (13), Kate (10), Moses (8), George (5), Rosina (2)*			
9	George Rogers	46	General labourer/builder	Kirtlington
	Theresa Rogers	40		Marston
	+ *Leah (10)*			

11	George Simpson	31	Carpenter		Oxford
	Sarah Simpson	28			Oxford
	+ Mildred (5), Edith (3), Hubert (1), Ernest (2 weeks)				
13	Alfred Goodall	36	Tailor		Oxford
	Clara Goodall	38			Wolvercote
	+ Georgina (10), Frederick (7), Florence (4), Elsie (2), Lilian (8 months)				
15	Walter Collett	36	Carpenter		Wolvercote
	Elizabeth Collett	38			Brackley
	Luke Hearn	65	Butcher		Brackley
	+ Albert (10), Emily (6)				
17	Emily Brooks (single)	23	Laundress (unmarried)		Oxford
	Albert Clarke	42	Railway porter (widower)		Southmoor
	Frank Clarke	15	Pupil teacher		Oxford
	+ William Brooks (1), Mabel Randall (2, Emily's niece), William Clarke (10)				
19	Joseph Shirley	29	Railway porter		Kidlington
	Jane Shirley	26			Kingham
	Charles Kench	70	Gardener (lodger)		Oxford
	+ Sarah (3), Mary (2), Joseph (8 months)				
21	Arthur Taylor	30	Bricklayer		Somerton
	Martha Taylor	28			Oxford
	Susan Miles	15	Domestic servant		Standlake
23	Robert Holloway	54	Engine driver		Sonning
	Mary Holloway	39			Thame
	Harry Holloway	15	Gardener		Watlington
	+ Kate (13), Lilian (11), Margaret (9), Frank (8), Mabel (6), Headland (3)				

31

25	Albert Parsons	27	Painter	Wells
	Emily Parsons	28		Oxford
	+ *Albert (7), Edith (4), Alice (2)*			
27	Benjamin Walker	34	Gardener	Penn Street
	Hannah Walker	34		Surrey
	John Hough	29	Carpenter	Warwick
	+ *Ernest (11), Harry (6), Rowland (3)*			
29	Edwin Judd	36	Gardener	Bucks
	Emily Judd	33		Wolvercote
31	William Doe	39	Printer (widower)	Oxford
	Evelyn Doe	15		Oxford
	+ *Winifred (13), William (12)*			
33	William Cox	47	Coal labourer	Walsall
	Hannah Cox	50		Oxford
	Francis Cox	22	College servant	Oxford
	Edward Cox	19	Fishmonger's assistant	Oxford
	George Cox	17	Rope maker's assistant	Oxford
	Ernest Cox	14	House boy	Oxford
35	George Attfield	29	Compositor	Surrey
	Catherine Attfield	29		Suffolk
	+ *Dorothy (3), William (3 months)*			
37	Charles Beesley	37	Printer	Oxford
	Elizabeth Beesley	36		Clifton Hampden
	+ *Florence (7), May (5), Harold (3)*			
39	John Bridgwater	40	Signalman	Oxford
	Charlotte Bridgwater	44		Oxford

41	Agabus Green	60	Builder's labourer	Botley
	Ann Green	58	Laundress	Oxford
	Annie Green	16	Domestic servant	Oxford
43	John Brain	35	Police constable	Westcott
	Rachel Brain	34		Oxford
	+ *Charles (5)*			
45	Christopher Gardiner	39	Joiner	Oxford
	Mahala Gardiner	30		Lincolnshire
	+ *Charles (8), Christopher (6), Mahala (5), Minnie (3), Alice (2 months)*			
47	Arthur Bell	28	Coachman	Staffordshire
	Elizabeth Bell	30		Staffordshire
	+ *George (4), Ada (3)*			
49	William Barnett	60	Jeweller	Birmingham
	Sarah Barnett	58		Birmingham
51	Harry Gosling	49	Wood turner	Oxford
	Mary Gosling	47		Oxford
	Alice Gosling	14		Oxford
	+ *Clara (12), Katherine (9)*			
53	Edwin Goddard	35	Police constable	Fencott
	Esther Goddard	34		Oakley
	+ *Amelia (8), Edwin (6), William (5), Thomas (2)*			
55	George Dunford	38	Groom and gardener	Dorset
	Harriett Dunford	38		Devon
	Amy Dunford	14		
	+ *George (5), Edith (3)*			
57	Alfred Webb	38	Carpenter/joiner	Iffley
	Helena Webb	32		Littlemore
	+ *Bessie (7), Charles (5), Agnes (3), John (1)*			

59	Vincent Saxton	44	Compositor	Wolvercote
	Phoebe Saxton	38		Thrupp
	Florence Saxton	18	Photographic apprentice	Oxford
	Edward Saxton	15		Oxford
	+ *Cyril (11), Kenneth (9), Herbert (7), Wallace (5), Leslie (3), Avis (1), and a new-born son*			
61	John Barbrough	57	Farmer's labourer	Iffley
	Sarah Barbrough	49		Oxford
	Mary Barbrough	18	General domestic servant	Oxford
	+ *Frederick (12), Thomas (6)*			
63	William Brooks	25	Cabinet maker's porter	Oxford
	Rose Brooks	25		Hinksey
	William Curtis	67	(Ret'rd gardener; widower; lodger)	Charlbury
	Harry Bunting	17	Waterman (lodger)	Hinksey
	+ *Agnes (9), James (1)*			
65	George Stagg	46	Carpenter/joiner	Somerset
	Sarah Stagg	43		Somerset
	Alice Stagg	19	Improver to dressmaker	Somerset
	Isaac Stagg	14		Bristol
	+ *George (13), Frances (10)*			
67	Richard Brooks	39	Type founder	Oxford
	Sarah Brooks	34		Banbury
	+ *Richard (7), Eveline (6), Lilian (4), Blanche (1)*			
69	William Scroggs	38	Signalman on GWR	Barton
	Eliza Scroggs	36	Tailoress	Oxford
	Charlotte Borton	33	(William's sister)	Headington
	Walter Howkins	21	Printer's machine minder (Eliza's brother)	Oxford
	Thomas Scroggs	15	Compositor's apprentice	Oxford

71	James Read	35	Baker	Oxford
	Thurza Read	37		Oxford
	Florence Read	18	Domestic servant	Oxford
	+ *George (11), Ernest (8), Cecil (6), Beatrice (3)*			
73	Antony Harris	55	Farmer	Oxford
	Sarah Harris	48		Oxford
	Ada Jane Best	18	Domestic servant (niece)	Oxford
2	Elias Nelms	65	Cab and fly proprietor (widower)	Berkeley
	Mary Butler	58	Housekeeper (widow)	Hasley
	Kate Butler	21	(Elias' niece)	Hasley
	Mary Flury	52		Berkeley
	Robert Flury	57	Coachman (Elias' nephew)	Brompton
4	John Woodford	38	Butcher	Kidlington
	Alice Woodford	30		Oxford
	+ *Edward (10), Archibald (8), Harry (7), Horace (6), Evelyn (2)*			
6	Harry Bishop	35	Waiter at inn	Oxford
	F.A.	34		Kidlington
	Elizabeth Kilby	27	(Widow; Harry's sister)	Oxford
	Mrs Brimfield	72	(Lodger; living on own means)	Oxford
	+ *Alice (5), and 2 unnamed infants*			
8	Thomas Church	32	Coachman/groom	Kent
	Emma Church	38		Oxford
10	Henry Margetts	54	Coke merchant	Oxford
	Sarah Margetts	49		Oxford
	Mary Margetts	18	Mother's help	Oxford
	John Margetts	15	Errand boy	Oxford
	Lionel Margetts	13	Errand boy	Oxford
	+ *May (10), Thomas (8)*			

12	Eli Collins	50	Lathrender	Woburn Sands
	Ann Collins	50	Domestic in own house	Aspley Green
	George Collins	28	Lathrender	Woburn Sands
	Charles Collins	24	Lathrender	Woburn Sands
	Eli Collins	19	Labourer	Lower Heyford
	Adam Collins	15	Gentleman's servant	Lower Heyford
	+ *Emma (10), Thomas (8)*			
14	Benjamin Higgs	28	Journeyman baker	Oxford
	Sarah Higgs	28		Leamington Spa
	+ *Forence (9), Benjamin (7), George (3), Frank (3)*			
16	George Brown	57	Builder's labourer	Oxford
	Jane Brown	50	Laundress	Oxford
	Mary Green	28	Hyde's factory (Jane's daughter)	Oxford
	James Green	15	Printer at Clarendon Press (Jane's son)	Oxford
	Frederick Brown	15	Servant at the Mitre	Oxford
	+ *Louisa Green (10, Jane's daughter)*			
18	Charles Pittman	24	Coach trimmer	Oxford
	Elizabeth Pittman	31		Oxford
20	William Gunn	24	Postman	Oxford
	Elizabeth Gunn	24		Westmoreland
22	Philip Martin	36	Compositor	Somerset
	Ellen Martin	34		Oxford
	+ *Thomas (5), William (1 month)*			
24	William Tross	41	Coachman	Isle of Wight
	Mary	33		Isle of Wight
	+ *William (11), Gertrude (8), Herbert (6), Harry (3), Jessie (6 months)*			

26	John Bridgen	40	House furnisher's salesman	Chichester
	Emily Bridgen	41		London
	+ Gertrude (9), Hannah (5)			
28	William Morse	43	Painter (invalid)	Faringdon
	Maria Morse	47	Sick nurse	Oxford
	William Morse	18	Tailor's apprentice	Oxford
	Ellen Morse	14		
	+ Francis (13), Edward (10), Thomas (8)			
30	Albert Tuffery	25	Gardener	Kidlington
	Clara Tuffery	22		Warwick
	Francis Tuffery	19	Greengrocer's porter	Kidlington
32	Henry Harris	39	Painter	Oxford
	Sarah Harris	30		Worcester
	William Harris	16	Printer's labourer	Oxford
	+ Jane (10)			
34	William Talbot	34	Coachman/groom	Woburn Sands
	Fanny Talbot	34		Worcester
	+ Ethel (6), Mary (2)			
36	Albert Money	22	Bricklayer	Oxford
	Mary Money	21		Oxford
	Richard Barron	85	Retired carter (Albert's father)	Tyso
	Charles Bond	24	Gardener (boarder)	Staffordshire
	+ Emily (1)			

38	John Mills	36	Gardener	Maidstone
	Elizabeth Mills	37		Stonesfield
	Hira Lal Kumar	28	Author/journalist (lodger; widower)	India
	+ *Harold (9), Violet (4)*			
40	Joseph Hicks	32	Coachman/groom	Berks
	Mary Hicks	30		Bucks
	+ *Norah (6), Ephraim (4), Florence (1)*			
42	George Gardner	46	Mason	Painswick
	Eliza Gardner	38		Swerford
	Eunice Gardner	17	Mother's help	Swerford
	+ *William (13), Olivia (10)*			
44	John Amos	35	Carpenter	Worcester
	Elizabeth Amos	31		Aldershot
	+ *John (13), Frederick (10), Alexander (5), Edwin (2 months)*			
46	Benjamin Lewis	33	Brewer	Poole
	Elizabeth Lewis	28		Headington
	+ *Benjamin (5), Edith (3), Francis (8 months)*			
48	Albert Timms	34	Painter	Oxford
	Frances Timms	36		Tackley
	+ *Henry (5)*			
50	John Judge	62	Carpenter	Ireland
	Hannah Judge	58	Sick nurse	Bicester
	Louisa Judge	19	Dressmaker	Oxford
	Harry Judge	14	Apprentice to hosier	Oxford
52	William Judge	28	Joiner	Oxford
	Ada Judge	28		Yorkshire
	+ *Edith (3)*			

54	Harry Burdon	38	General labourer	Eynsham
	Henrietta Burdon	33		Steeple Barton
	Alfred Burdon	72	Gardener (Harry's father)	Eynsham
	Ellen Summersford	49	Retired teacher (lodger)	Gloucester
	+ *Henrietta (1)*			
56	Elizabeth Ariss	47	Laundress (widow)	Oxford
	John Ariss	20	Wood carver	Oxford
	Sarah Newman	75	Retired laundress (Elizabeth's mother)	Nuneham
58	John Browjohn	43	Compositor	Somerset
	Annie Browjohn	39		Oxford
	John Browjohn	14		Oxford
	+ *Winifred (13), Ernest (11), Edith (9), Lewis (6), Oliver (8 months)*			
60	Moses Smith	34	Groom/coachman	Bladon
	Elizabeth Smith	34		Grendon
	+ *Emily (13), Elizabeth (10)*			
62	Charles May	38	Porter/shunter on the GWR	Bampton
	Frances May	52		Hampshire
	John Smith	34	Bricklayer's labourer (lodger)	Bicester
	Gertrude May	23	Domestic	
	+ *Frank (11)*			
64	Christopher Choldcroft	31	Hairdresser's assistant	Herts
	Laura Choldcroft	32		Norfolk
	+ *Bessie (10), Cecil (9), Linda (6), William (4), Christopher (3), Winifred (1)*			
66	Samuel Stevens	26	Joiner's machinist	Oxford
	Annie Stevens	24		Oxford
	Arthur Narraway	21	Greengrocer's assistant (boarder)	Marston
	Ernest Narraway	17	Greengrocer's assistant (boarder)	Summertown
	+ *Amy (5)*			

68	Edward Robinson	28	Groom/coachman	Wolvercote
	Matilda Robinson	38		Witney
	Frederic Holt	33	Pressman (widower)	Oxford
	+ *Frederic Holt (8), Vernon Holt (6), Beatrice Robinson (1)*			
70	Walter Walker	44	Shoemaker	Oxford
	Walter Walker	17	General labourer	Oxford
	Henry Walker	14	Shoemaker's apprentice	Oxford
	Eliza Archer	48	Housekeeper	Oxford
72	George Sadler	33	Stamper at Post Office	South Hinksey
	Ellen Sadler	33		Oxford
	+ *Ann (8), Alfred (6), Archibald (1)*			
74	Frank East	38	Wood merchant's assistant	Oxford
	Mary East	33		Oxford
	+ *Charles (6), Frank (4)*			
76	William Hill	25	Cabinet maker	Oxford
	Elizabeth Hill	27		Reading
78	Thomas Kench	24	Poulterer/fishmonger	Headington
	Edith Kench	22		Summertown
80	William Chappell	43	Coach wheeler	Greenwich
	Phillis Chappell	34		Deptford
	+ *William (12), Robert (11), Rose (10), Lillie (9), Daisy (7), Violet (6), Myrtle (5), Eva (4) Gladys (2), Sydney (7 months)*			
82	Charles Innes	31	Bricklayer	Cumnor
	Kate Innes	29		Roke
	Arthur Innes	23	Bricklayer's labourer	Cumnor
84	Albert Bassett	41	Gardener	Steeple Barton
	Elizabeth Bassett	40		Steeple Barton
	+ *Albert (4)*			

86	William Pearson	39	Waiter at inn	Middlesex
	Alice Pearson	31		Sussex
	+ *Philip (5), Alice (4), Frank (2), Ellen (1)*			
88	Harry Rose	29	Shunter	Leamington
	Emma Rose	31		Brill
	Frank Lovell	20	Brewer's storeman (boarder)	Brill
	George Hibbins	21	Groom (boarder)	Huntingdonshire
	+ *Alice (4), Harry (2)*			
90	John Gray	45	Brickyard labourer	Oxford
	Elizabeth Gray	48		Wolvercote
	Lydia Gray	17	Mother's help	Summertown
	James Bowler	46	Brickyard labourer (lodger)	Marston
	+ *Harry (12)*			

❧ Sources ☙

Elspeth Buxton and Catherine Robinson did the research for this booklet, and Catherine Robinson wrote the text. The following principal sources were used:

❦ The national Census for 1841, 1851, 1861, 1871, 1881, and 1891 (copies stored in Oxford City Library)

❦ Contemporary issues of *Jackson's Oxford Journal* and *The Oxford Times* (also in the City Library)

❦ Parish magazines and other documents from St Margaret's Church, and St Philip's and St James's Church (stored in the Bodleian Library)

❦ Documents from the archives of St John's College

❦ *North Oxford* by Tanis Hinchcliffe (published by Yale University Press, 1992)

❦ And (most valuable of all) the memories of Mrs Freda Andrews, Mr Bob Ayres, Mrs Mary Giles, Miss Florrie Goddard, Mrs Jessie Harding, Miss Molly Harris, Mrs Nora Surman, and Mrs Doris Thicke. Thanks are due to them, and to everyone else who has helped, especially Paul Kendall, who did the design.

The cover picture shows Police Constable Edwin Goddard with his two youngest children, Anne and Stan, outside their home at 53 Hayfield Road, c. 1912.

Centenary street party, September 1985, drawn by Christine Court. (The party was held a year too early, but the present authors kept their suspicions to themselves, and everyone had a good time.)

❦ Acknowledgements ❧

Thanks are due to the following, for permission to reproduce copyright material:

The family of Miss Florrie Goddard for the photograph on the cover.

The Anchor Inn for the line drawing of Dolly's Hut

The Bodleian Library for the line drawing of Aristotle's Well.

Oxfordshire County Council Department of Leisure and Arts: Library Services for the photograph of Hayfield Wharf by Henry Taunt.

Oxford University Press for the line drawing of the canal drawbridge by David Miller (from *Ramlin Rose: The Boatwoman's Story*, by Sheila Stewart, published in 1993).

The Public Records Office for the extract from the Census of 1891.

Christine Court for her drawing of the centenary street party